TRANSCRIPTIONS
PIANO

THELONIOUS
THE
BEST OF MONK

MW00669014

Photo: Frank Driggs Collection
Thelonious Monk at Minton's Playhouse, NYC 1948

ISBN 978-0-7935-8748-3

HAL•LEONARD®
CORPORATION
7777 W. BLUEMOUND RD. P.O. BOX 13819 MILWAUKEE, WI 53213

Visit Hal Leonard Online at
www.halleonard.com

THELONIOUS MONK BIOGRAPHY

Thelonious Sphere Monk was born on October 10, 1917 in Rocky Mount, North Carolina. When he was four, his family moved to San Juan Hill, New York. His sister was the first in the family to take piano lessons, and Monk would learn by looking over her shoulder. Soon after, Monk was playing the piano in church and performing in the Apollo Theater's Amateur Contests. His playing style was developed early on, with his fingers flat and level on the keys, influenced by pianist Mary Lou Williams.

In the early 1940s, Monk was playing as a sideman in groups led by Kenny Clarke, Dizzy Gillespie and Charlie Parker. He became house pianist at Minton's Playhouse in Harlem, which eventually led to his first recording with the house quartet in 1941 while Charlie Christian was making a guest appearance. In 1944 Monk's signature tune "'Round Midnight" was recorded by Cootie Williams. Three years later, he made his first recordings under his own name for the Blue Note label. Between 1947 and 1952, Monk's output on the label would include recordings of the songs "Evidence," "Criss Cross," "Humph" and "Thelonious". These songs were the first indication of Monk's unique style of writing.

In 1951, Monk was arrested for narcotics and had his cabaret card taken from him, prohibiting him from working in New York nightclubs. He received a recording contract from Prestige Records in 1952, which lasted three years. During this period he recorded "Little Rootie Tootie", a song dedicated to his son, as well as his own eccentric version of "Smoke Gets in Your Eyes". Ultimately, the records didn't fare as well as other Prestige artists, such as Miles Davis and the Modern Jazz Quartet. Because of low sales, in 1955 Prestige Records sold his record contract to Riverside Records. This marked the beginning of a pivotal recording period in Monk's career. While at Riverside, Monk recorded such acclaimed albums as *Brilliant Corners*, *Thelonious Himself*, and *Thelonious Monk with John Coltrane*. While his unique style brought about controversy among jazz critics, these records established Monk as a composer and player.

By 1957, Thelonious Monk was allowed to play in nightclubs again. His first performance back was with a quartet at New York's Five Spot. This group featured John Coltrane, Wilbur Ware and Shadow Wilson, bringing even more attention to his music. He began to tour on a regular basis in both the U.S. and Europe. One concert in particular was a 1959 performance at New York's Town Hall, where a 10-piece orchestra performed Monk standards in expanded arrangements by Hall Overton. His rising popularity landed him on the cover of Time magazine in 1964, a rarity for a jazz musician.

In 1970, Monk disbanded his group. He went on to play with an all-star group in 1971-72 called the Giants of Jazz, which featured Dizzy Gillespie, Kai Winding, Sonny Stitt, Al McKibbon and Art Blakey. He also went on to make what would be some of his last recordings for the Black Lion label in 1971. It was after this that Monk suddenly decided to retire. Except for some festival appearances in 1975 and 1976, he spent his final years in seclusion at the home of Baroness Pannonica de Koenigswarter, a lifelong friend and patron. In 1982, Thelonious Monk died after suffering from a stroke at the age of 64.

THELONIOUS MONK

Bemsha Swing

By Thelonious Monk and Denzil Best

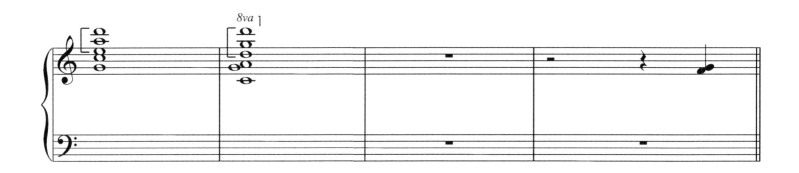

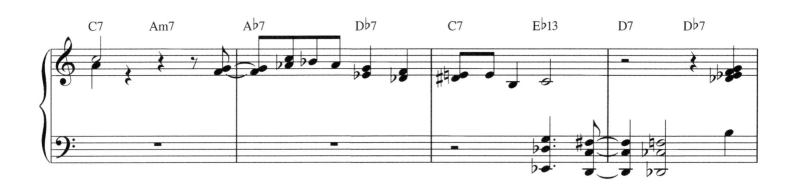

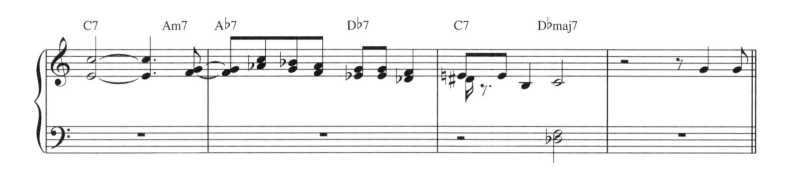

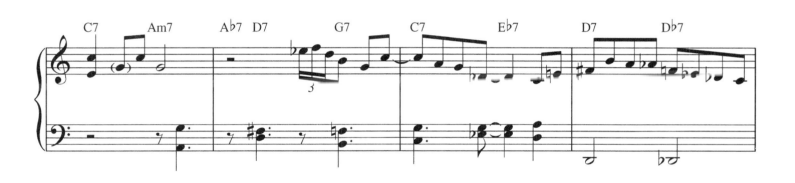

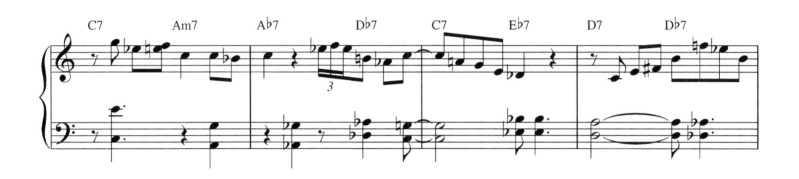

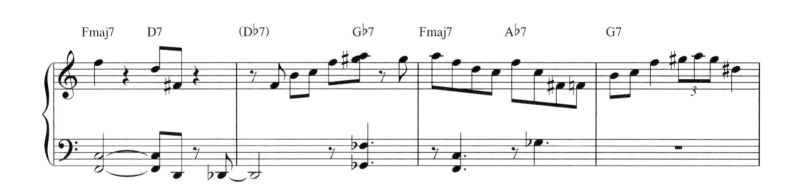

bass out for most of this chorus and all of the next chorus

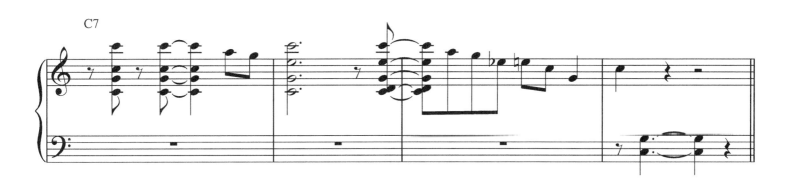

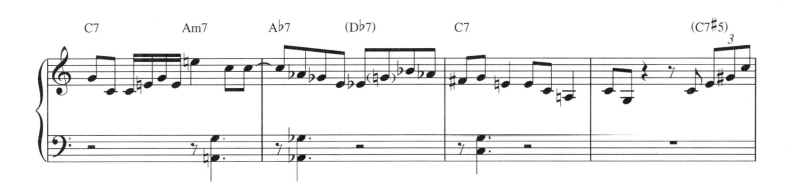

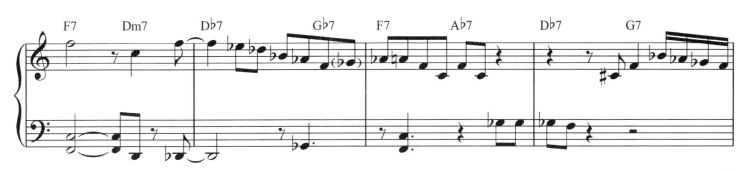

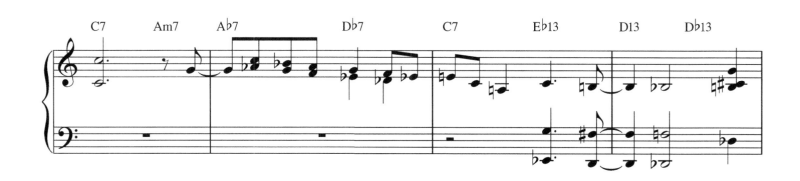

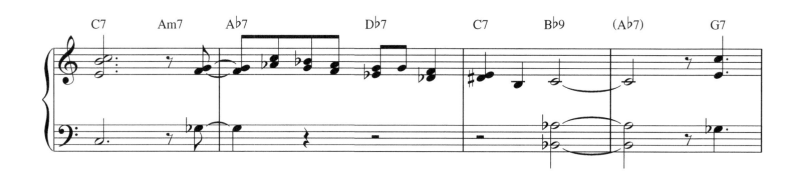

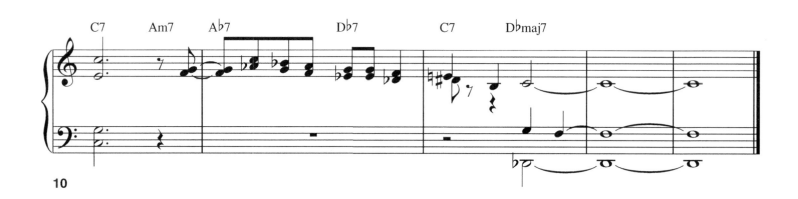

Blue Monk

By Thelonious Monk

Moderate Swing ♩ = 134

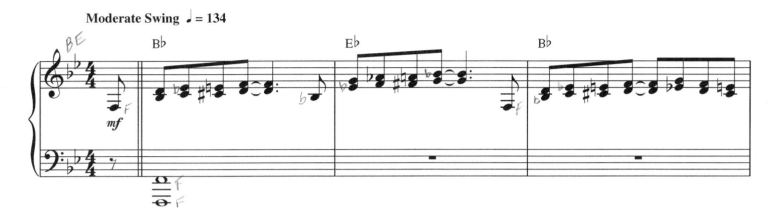

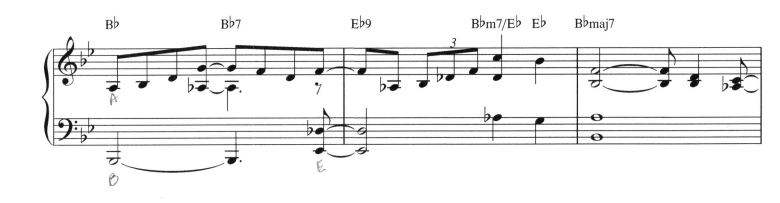

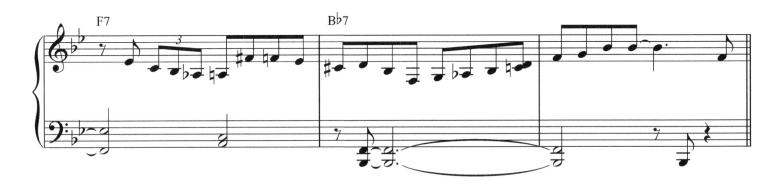

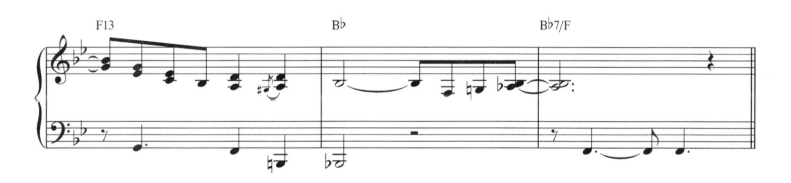

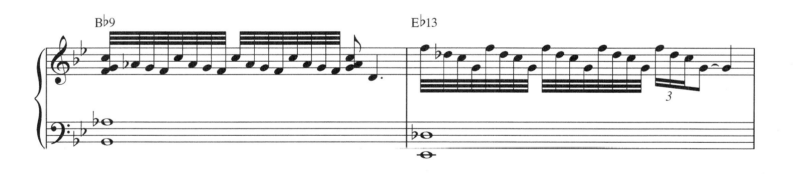

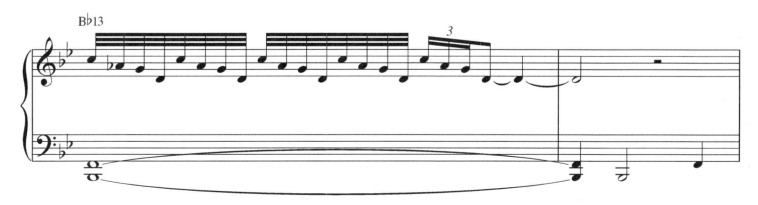

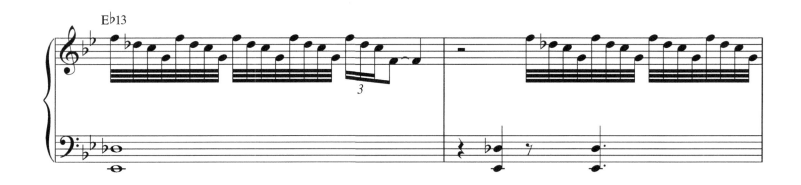

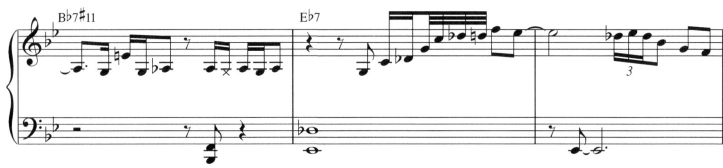

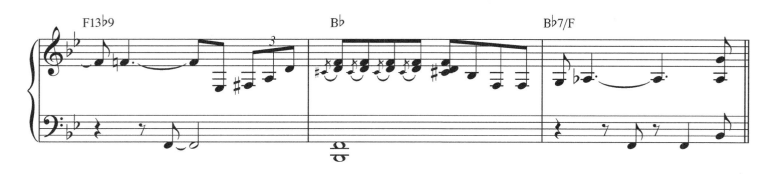

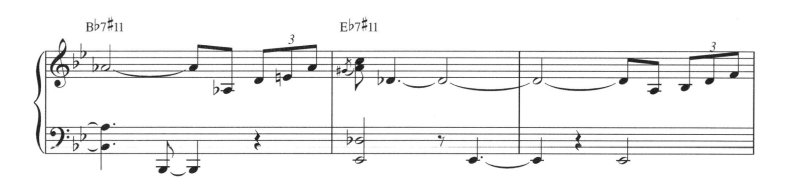

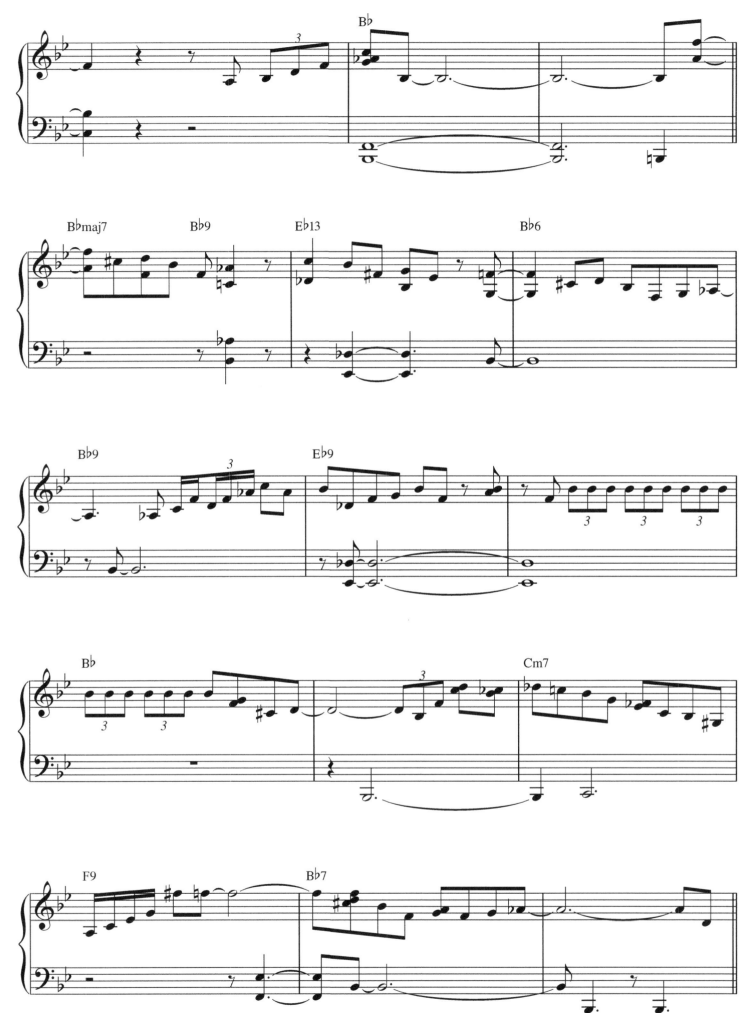

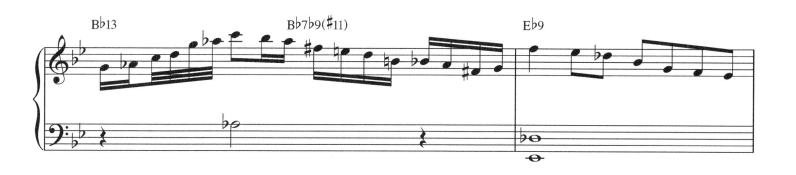

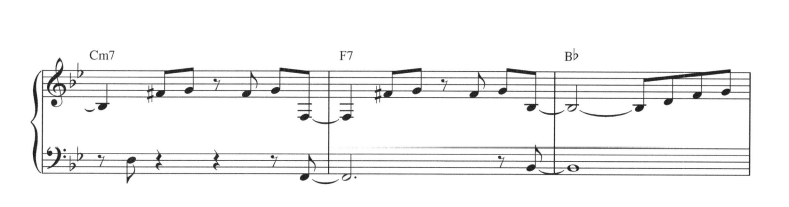

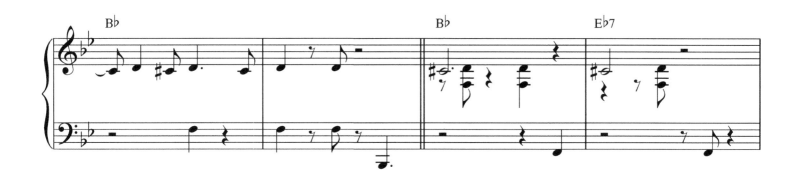

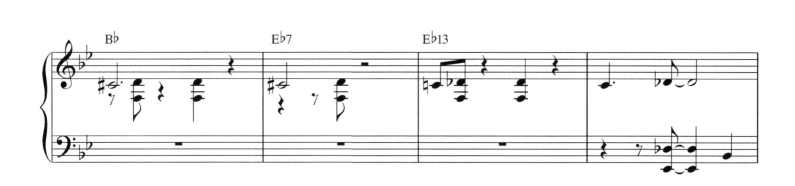

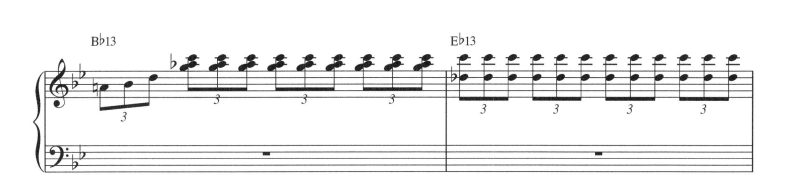

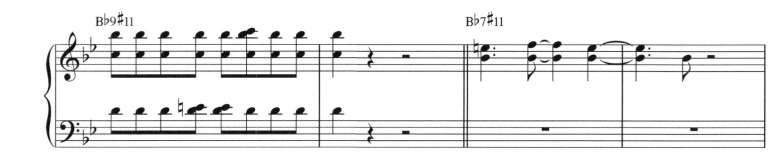

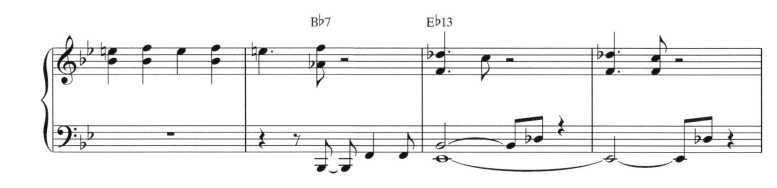

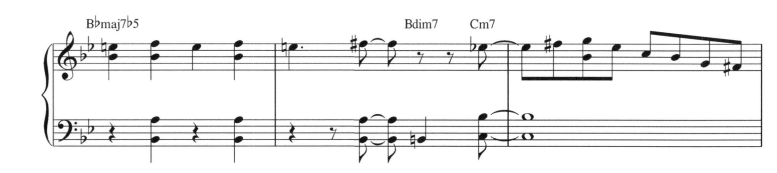

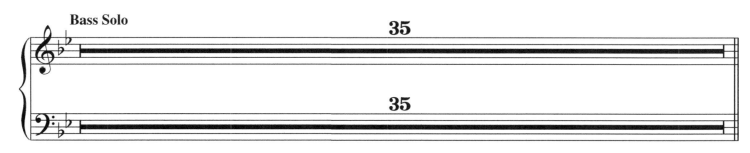

Drum Solo

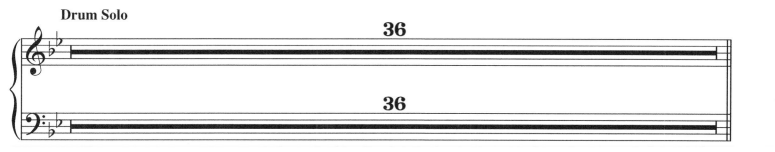

36

36

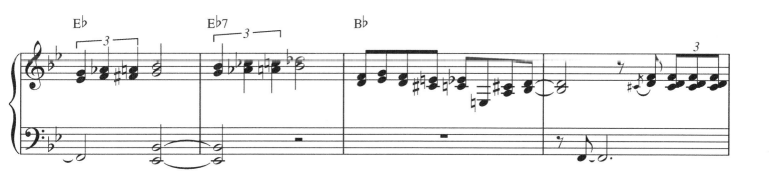

23

Boo Boo's Birthday

By Thelonious Monk

24

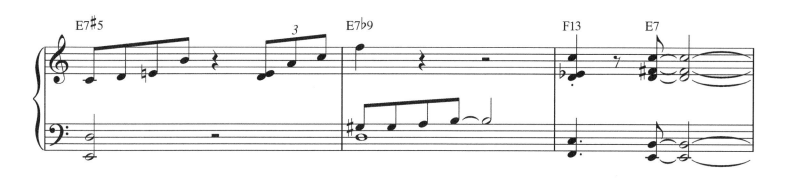

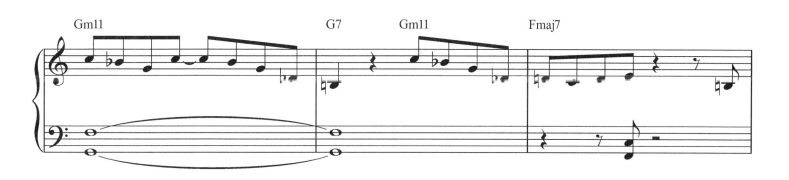

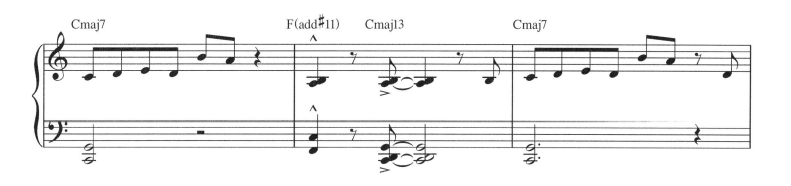

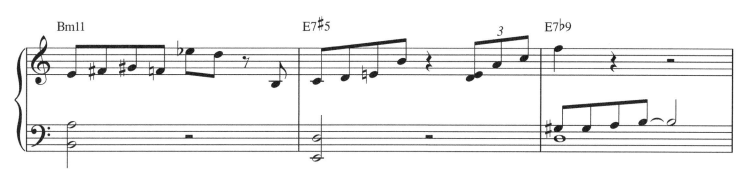

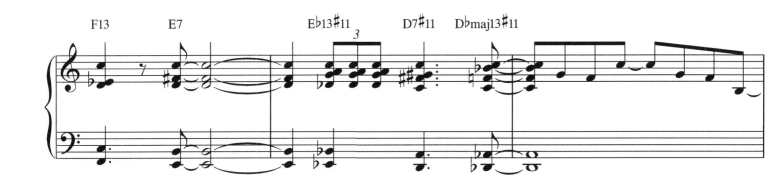

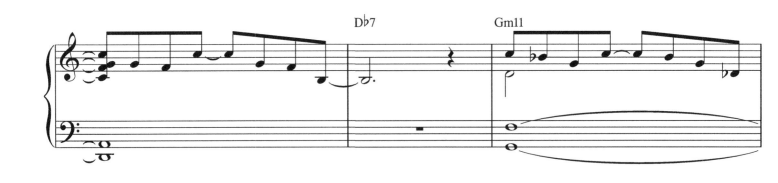

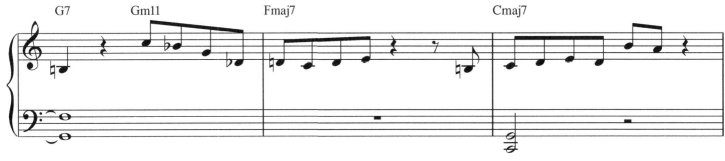

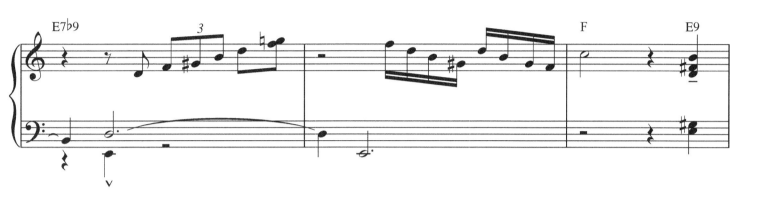

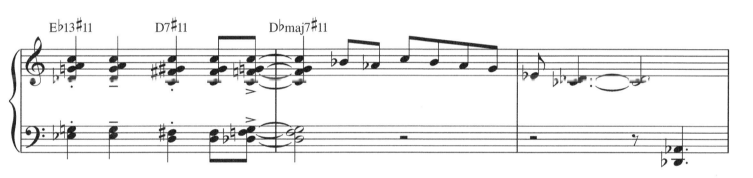

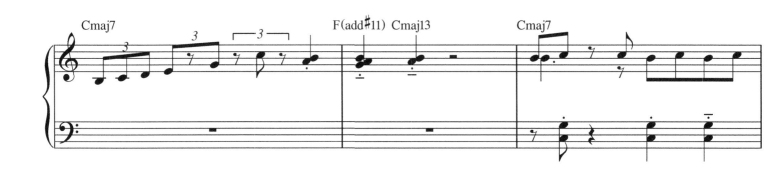

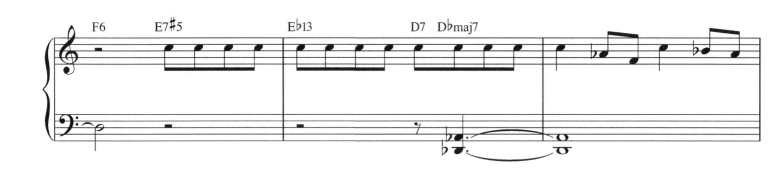

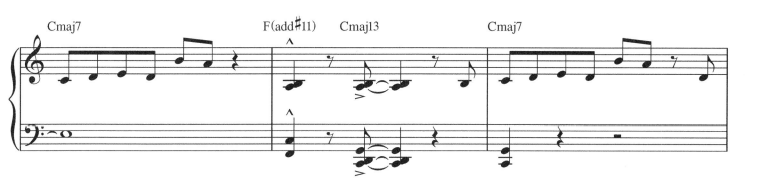

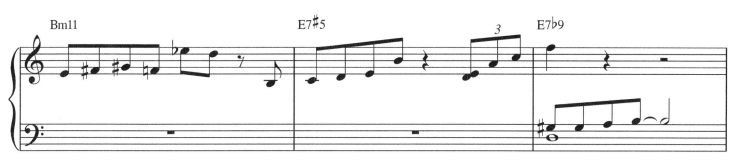

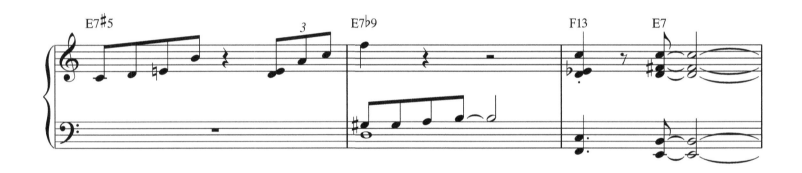

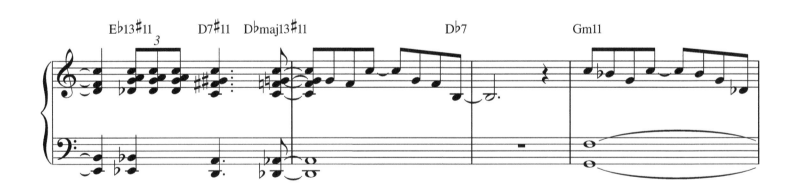

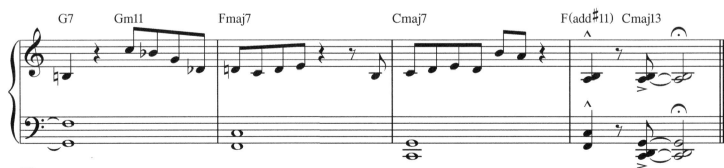

Criss Cross

By Thelonious Monk

Epistrophy

By Thelonious Monk and Kenny Clarke

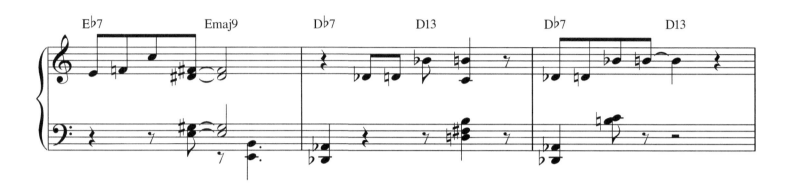

Piano Solo

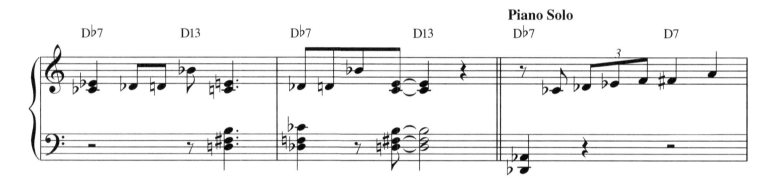

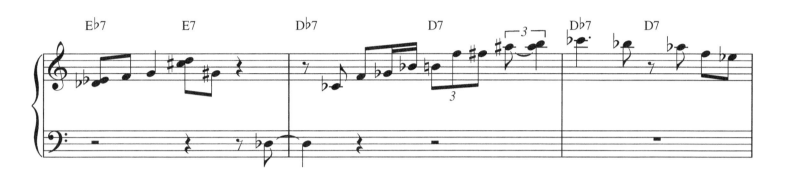

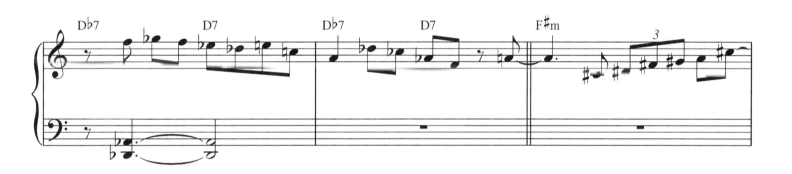

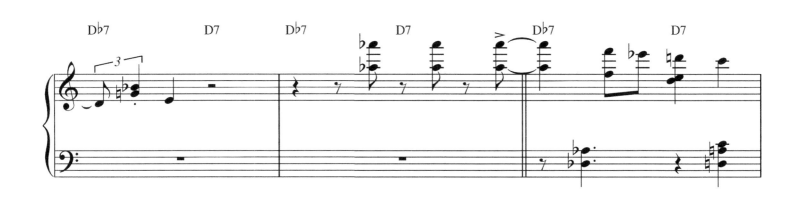

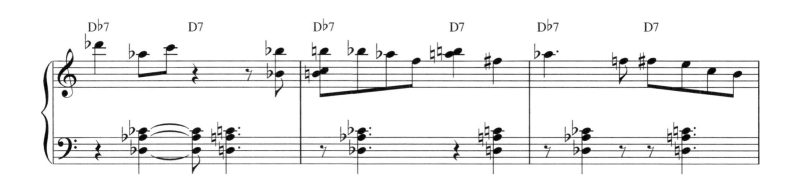

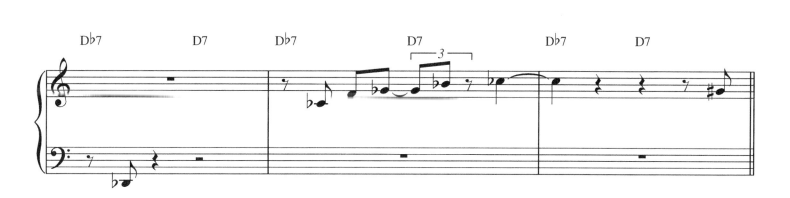

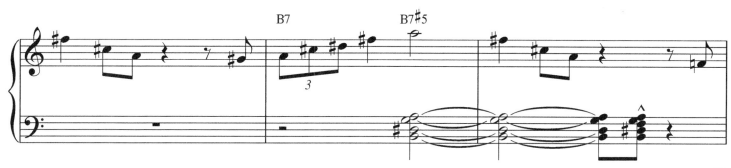

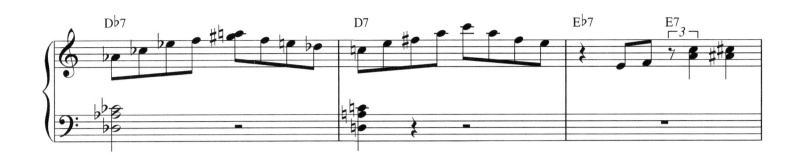

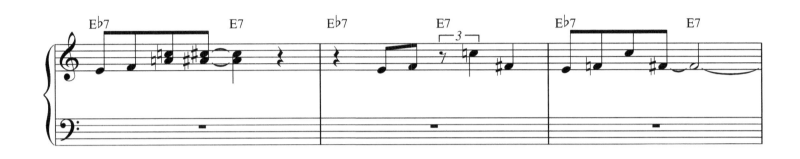

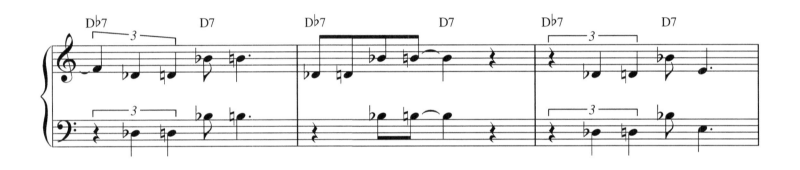

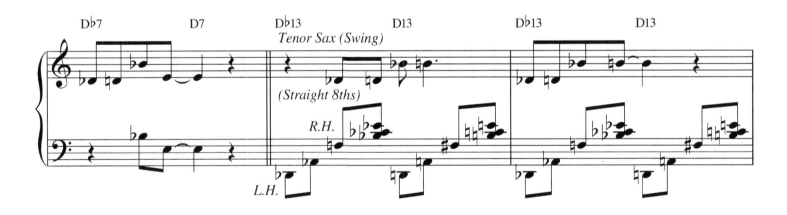

44

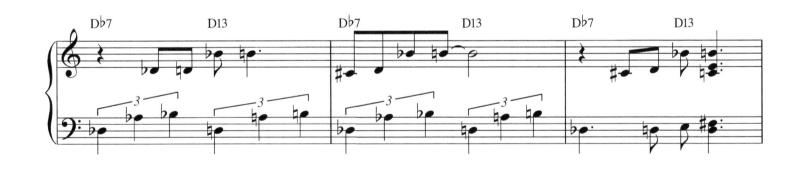

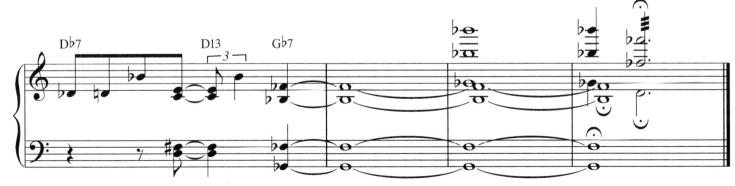

I Mean You

By Thelonious Monk and Coleman Hawkins

Medium Swing

Piano Intro

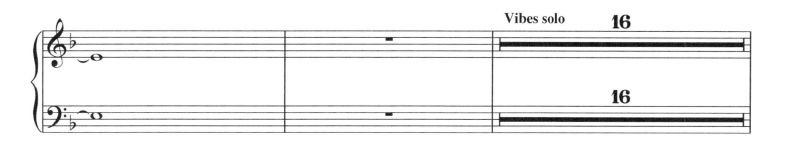

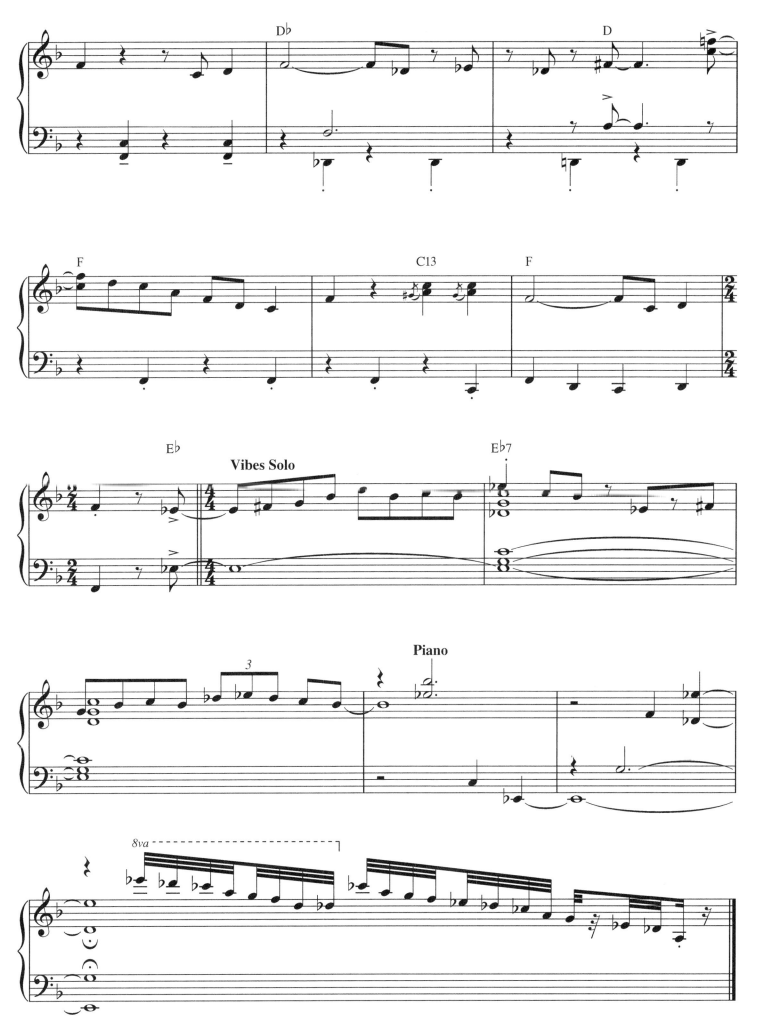

In Walked Bud

By Thelonious Monk

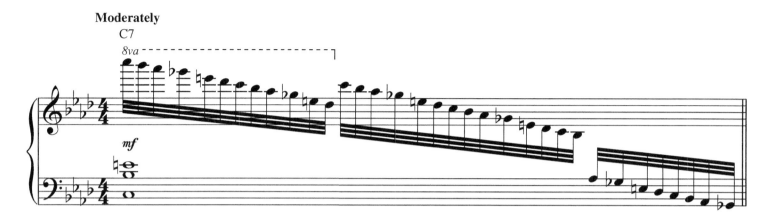

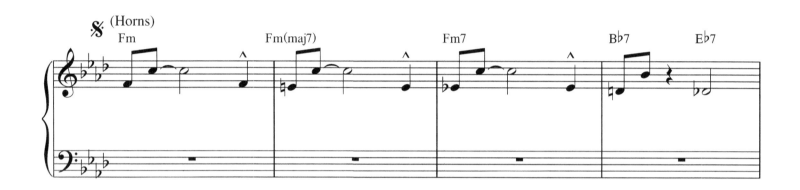

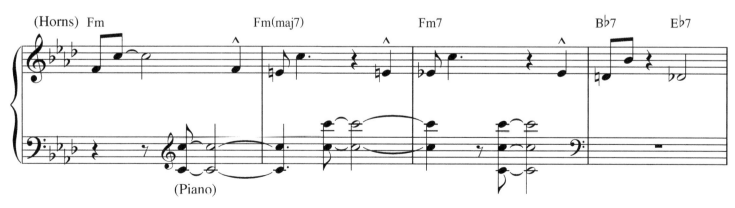

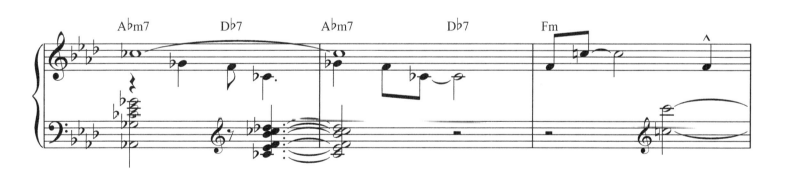

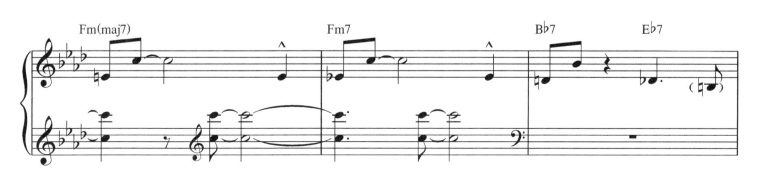

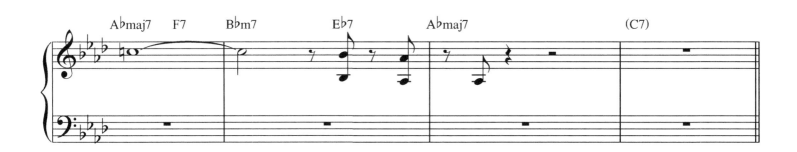

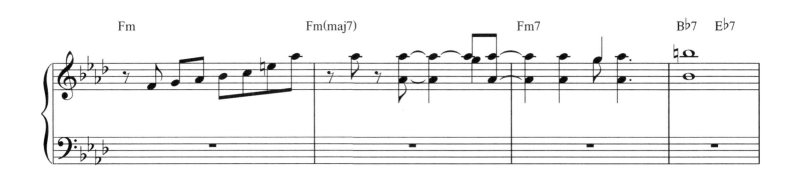

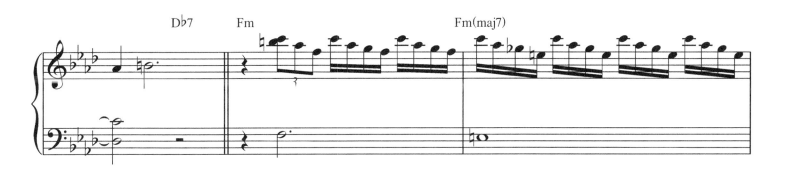

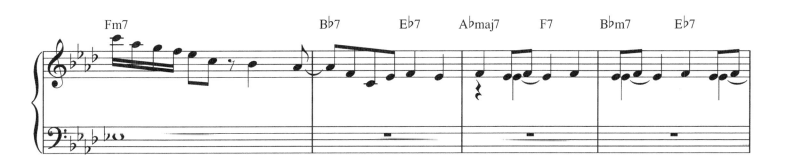

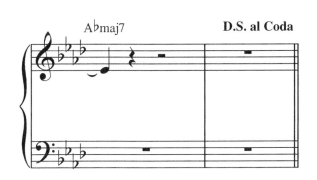

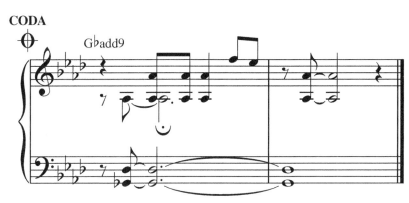

Let's Cool One

By Thelonious Monk

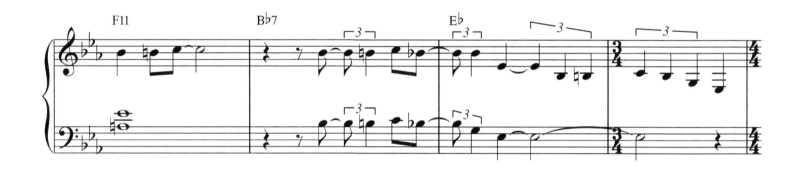

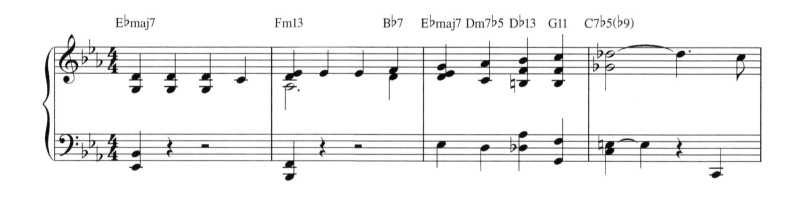

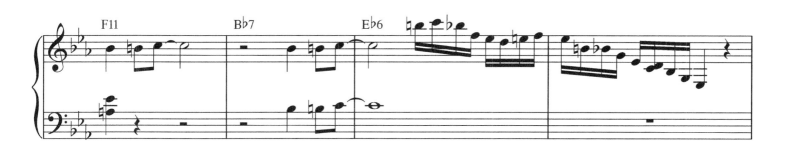

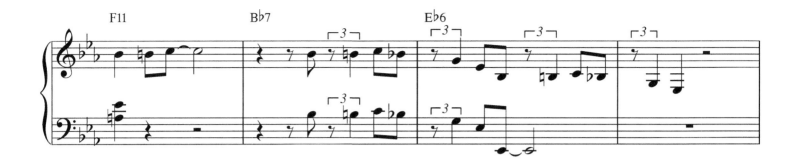

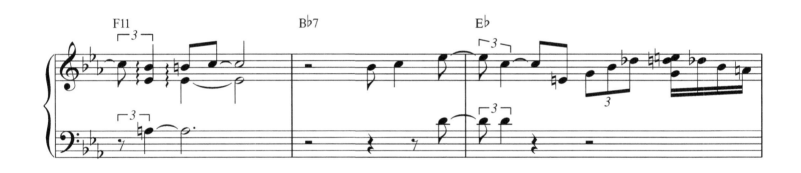

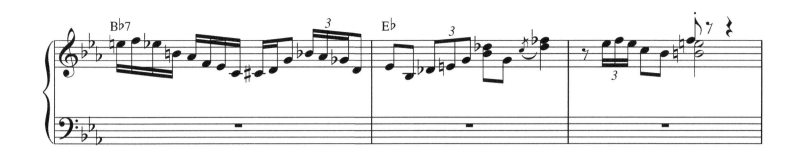

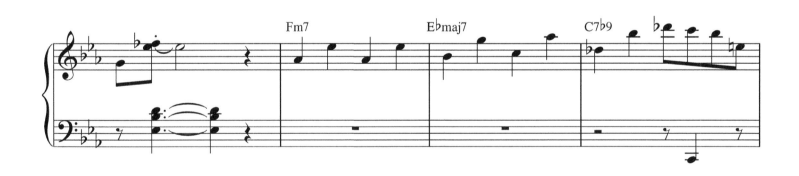

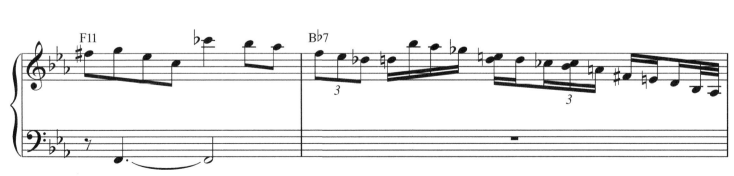

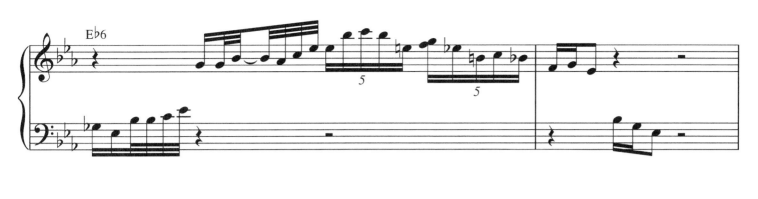

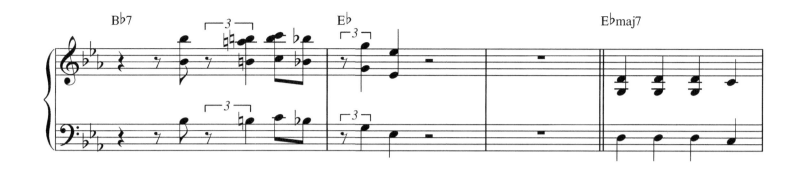

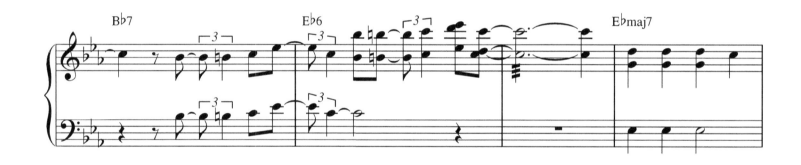

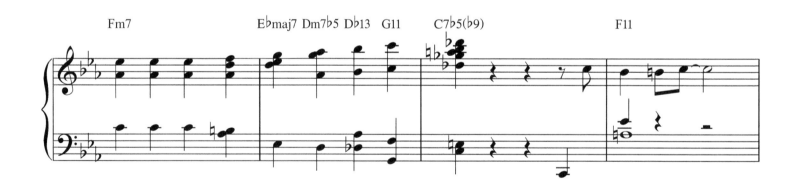

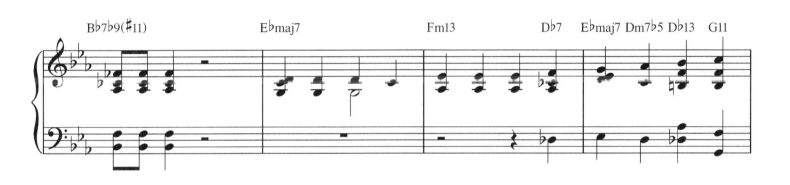

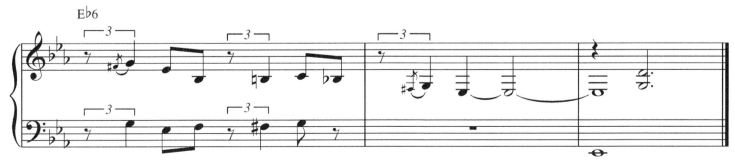

Monk's Dream

By Thelonious Monk

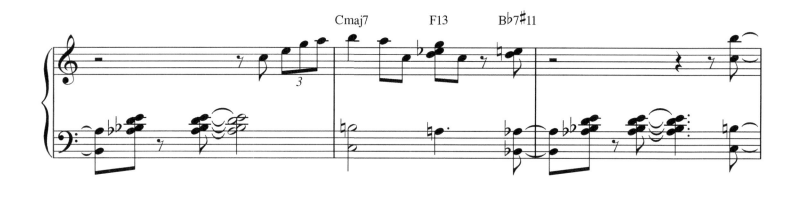

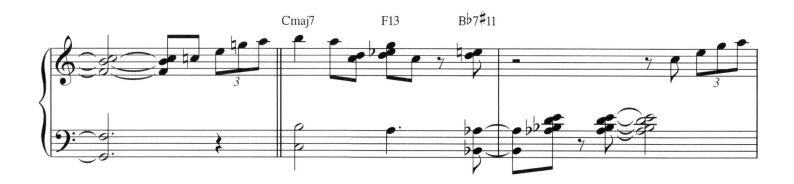

Nutty

By Thelonious Monk

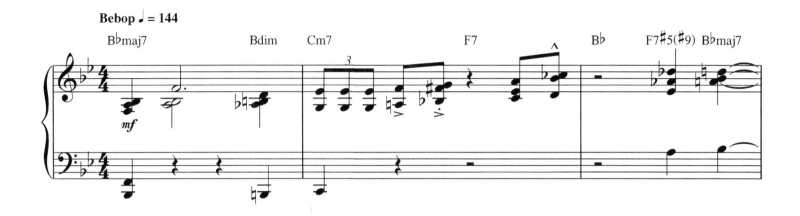

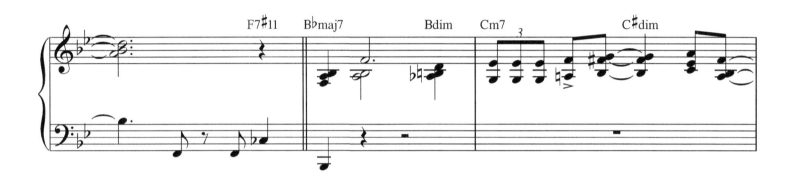

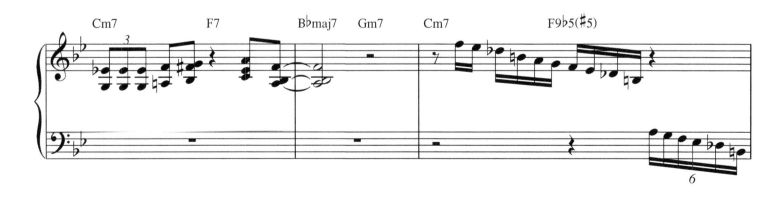

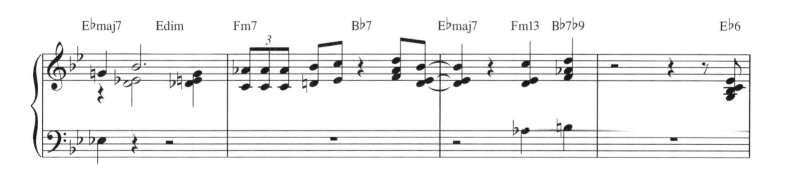

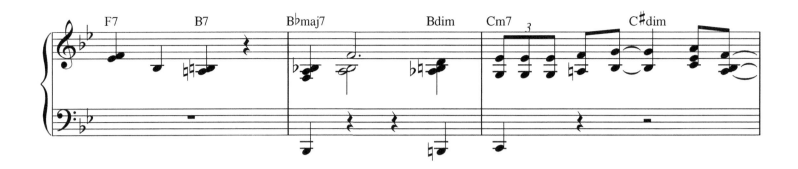

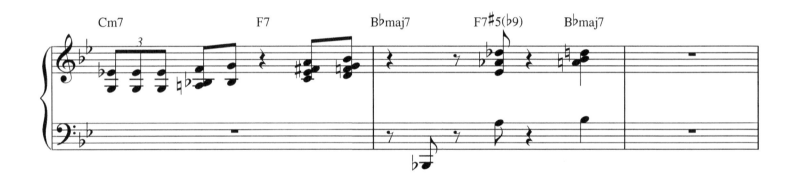

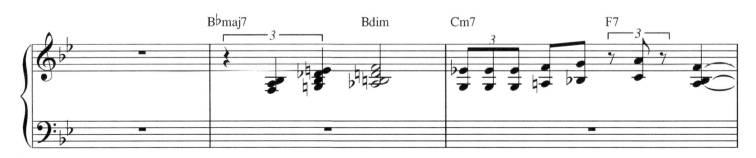

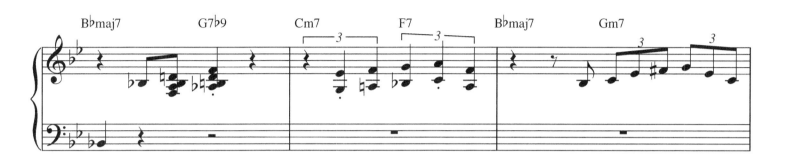

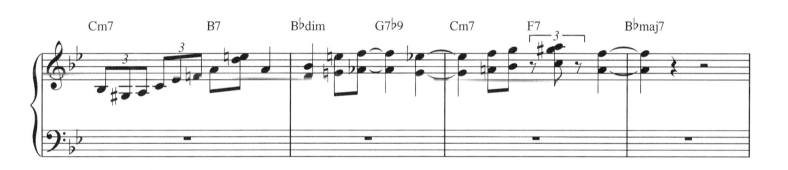

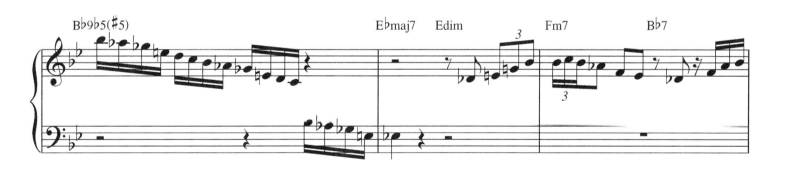

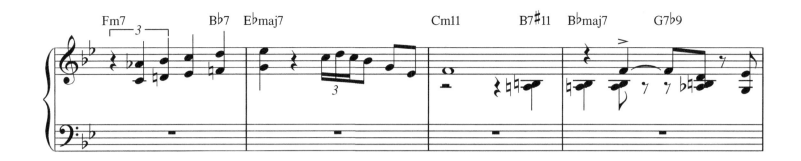

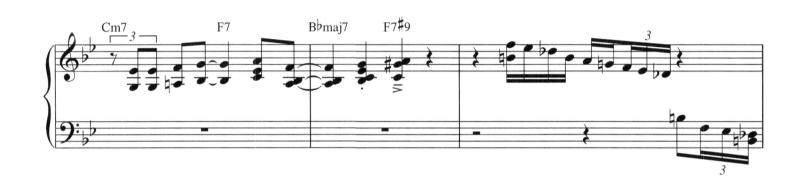

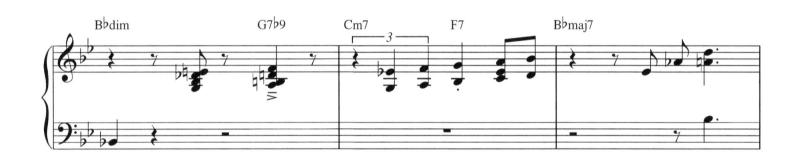

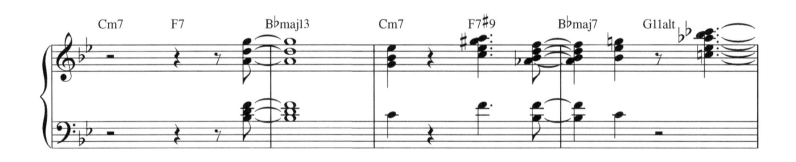

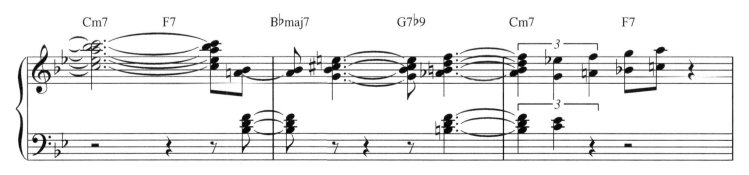

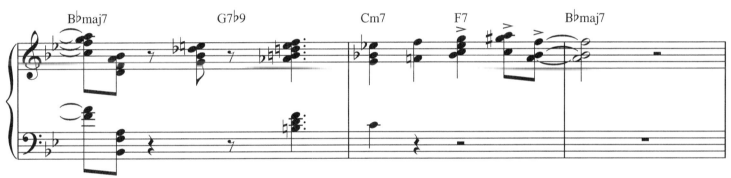

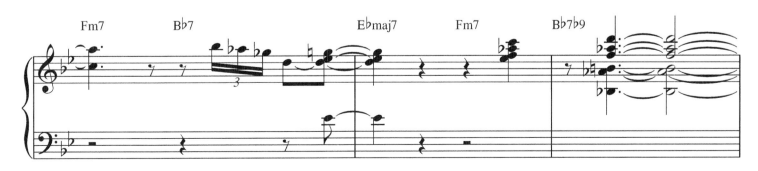

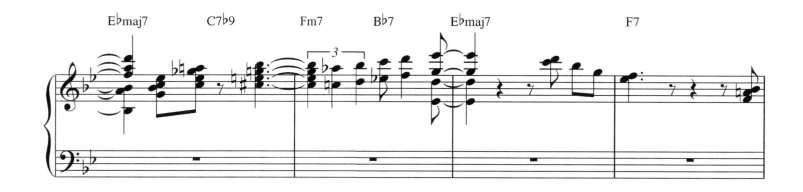

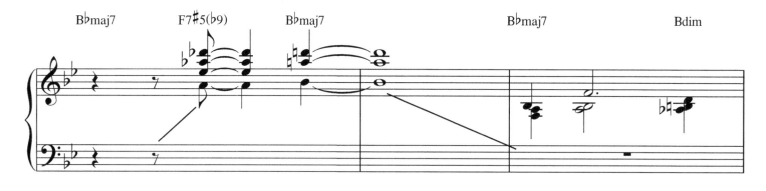

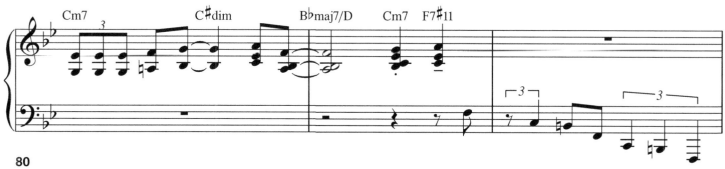

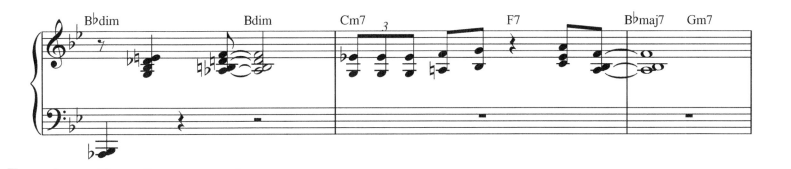

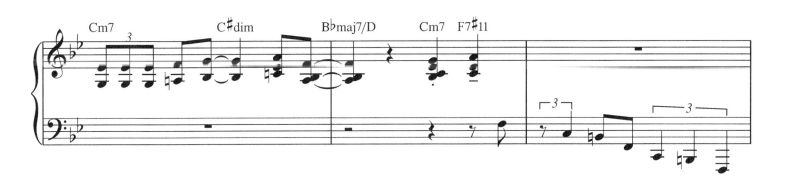

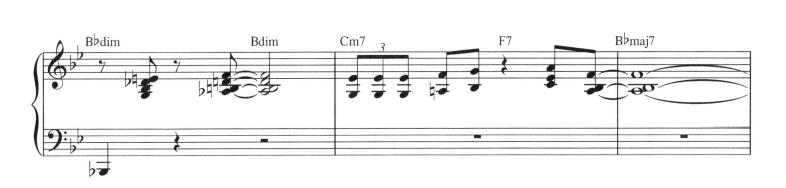

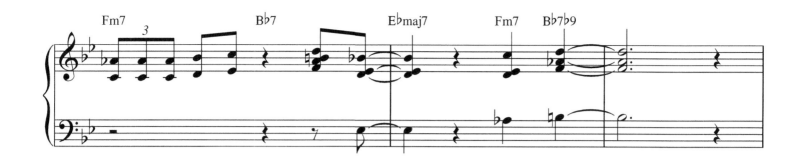

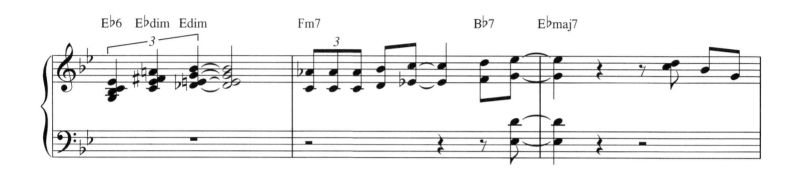

Off Minor

By Thelonious Monk

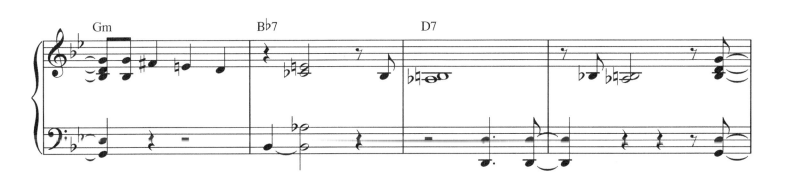

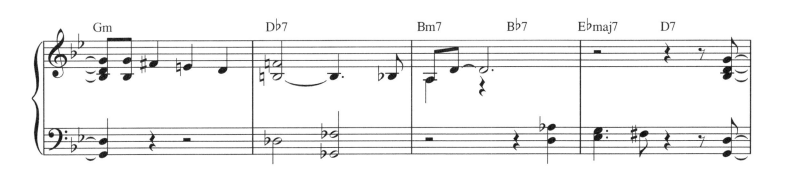

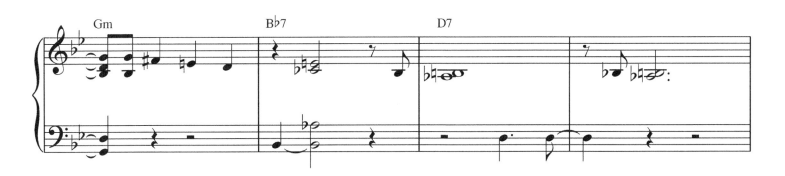

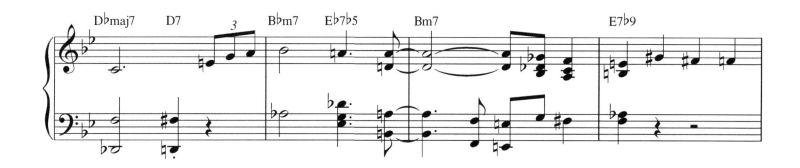

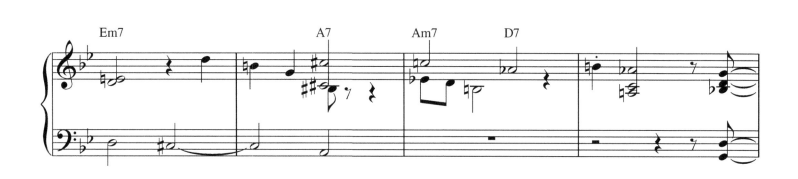

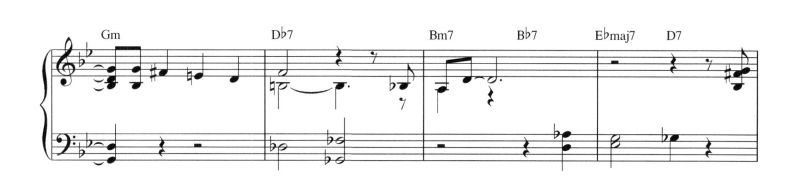

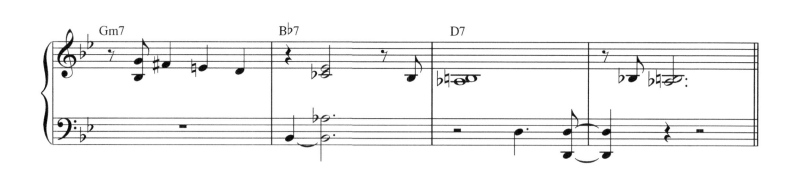

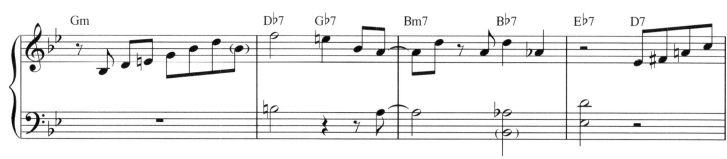

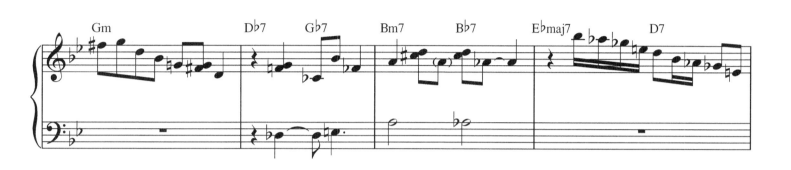

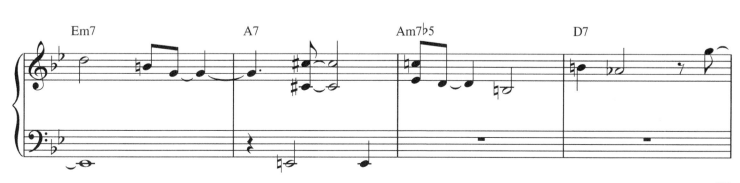

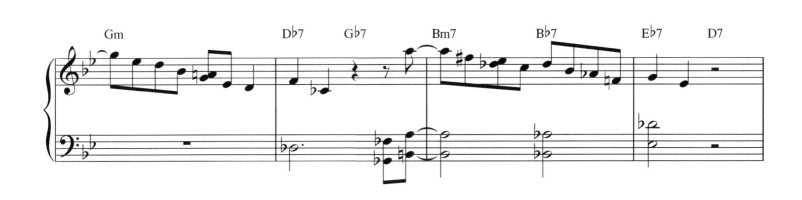

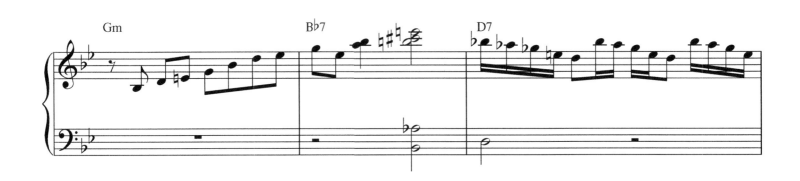

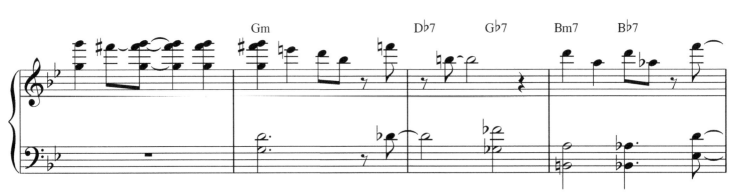

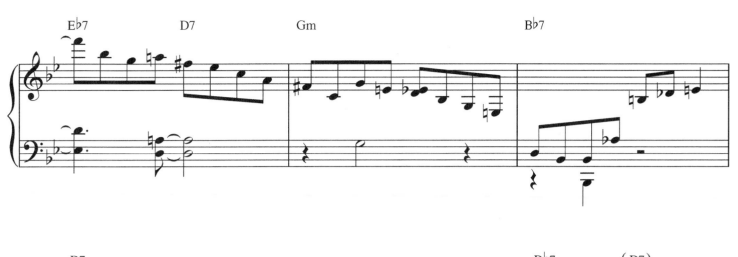

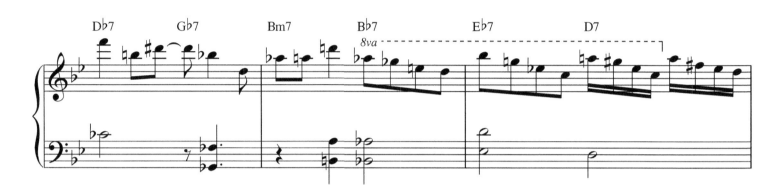

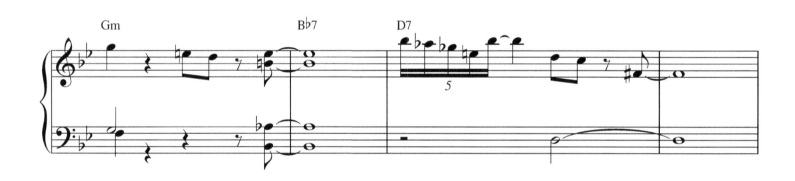

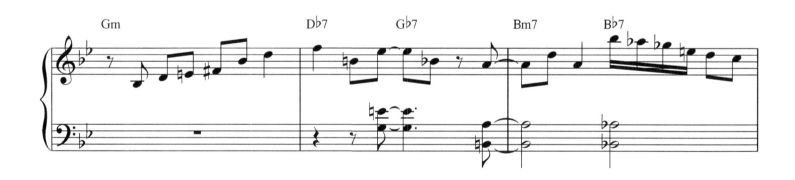

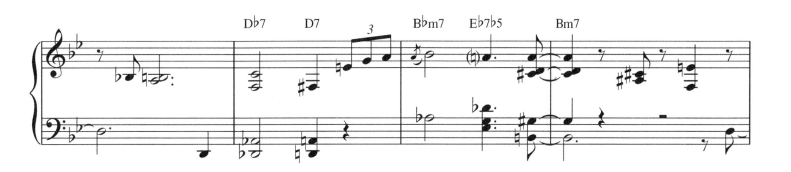

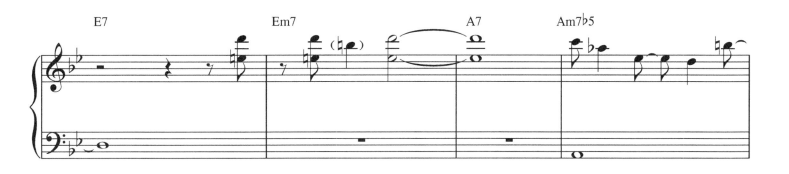

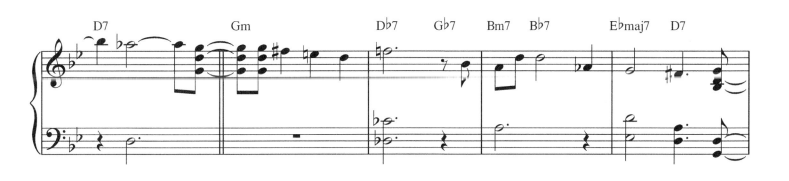

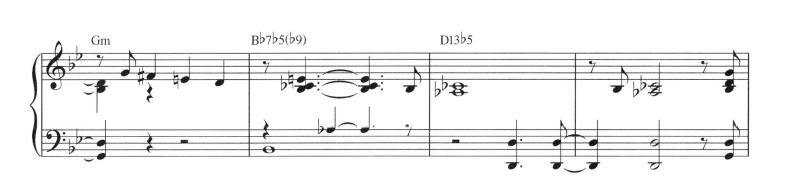

Rhythm-a-ning

By Thelonious Monk

Ruby, My Dear

By Thelonious Monk

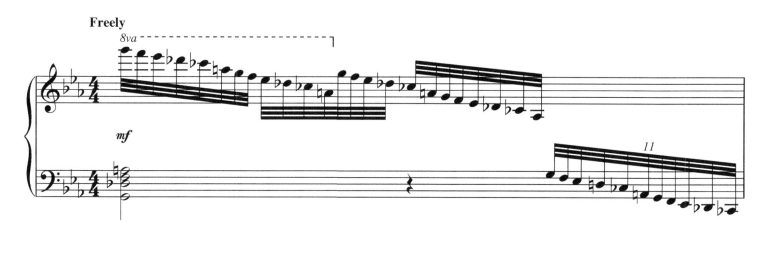

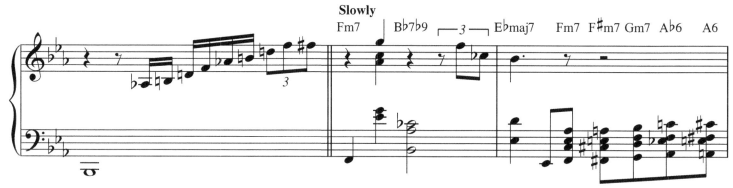

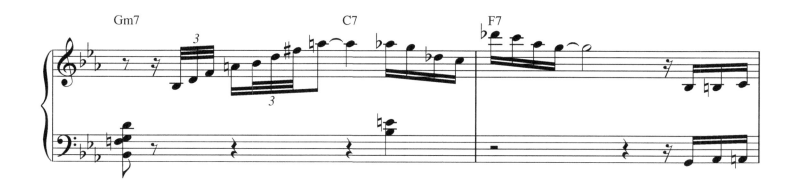

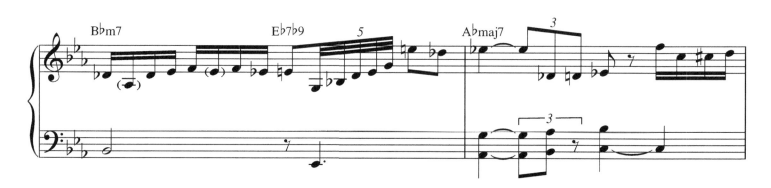

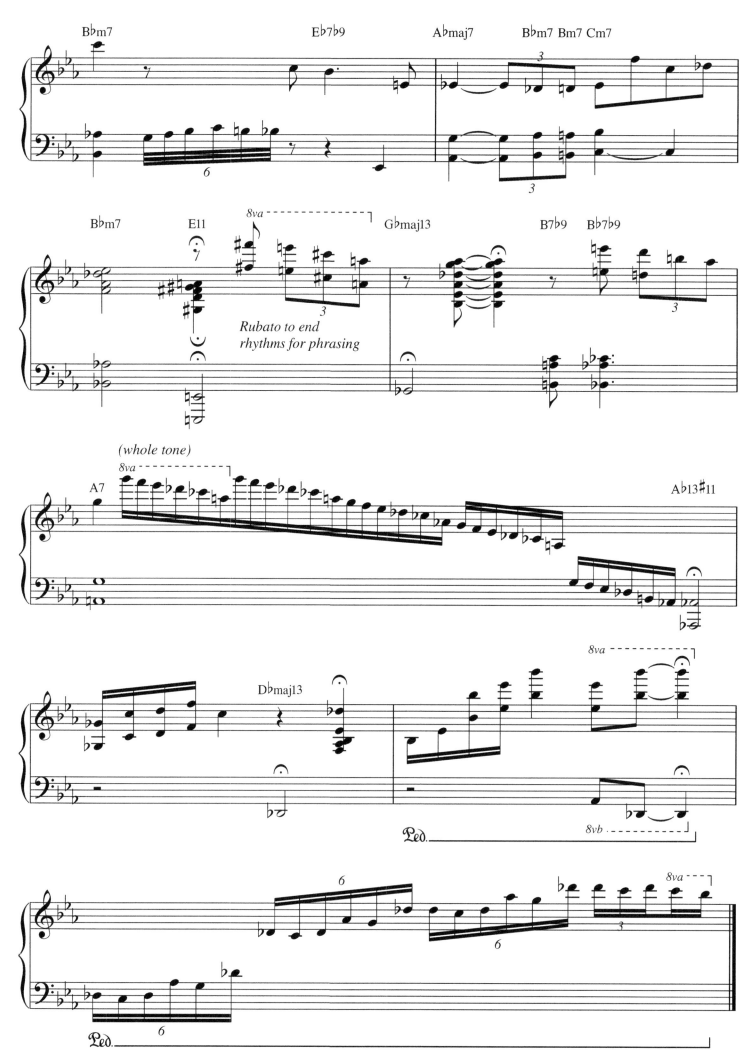

Rubato to end
rhythms for phrasing

(whole tone)

Straight No Chaser

By Thelonious Monk

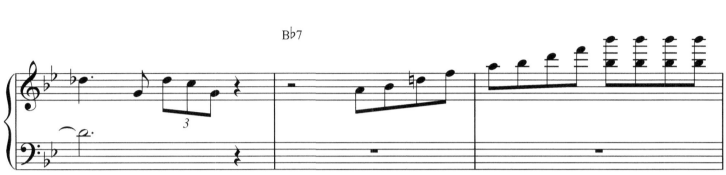

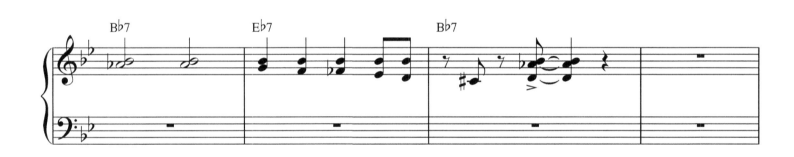

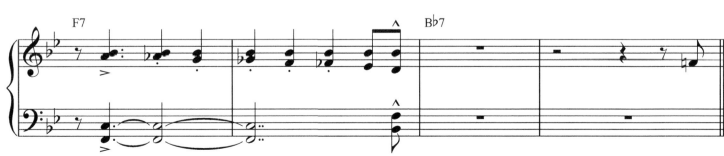

106

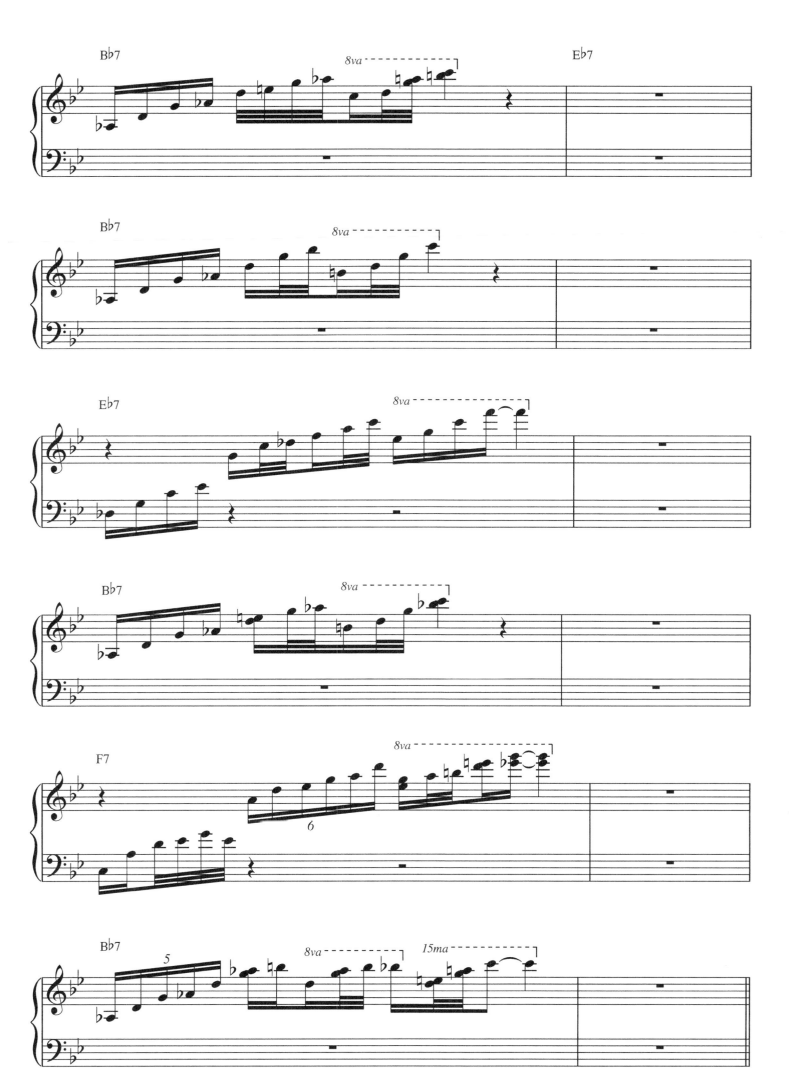

Well You Needn't

(It's Over Now)

English Lyric by Mike Ferro
Music by Thelonious Monk

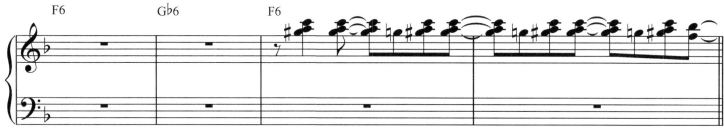

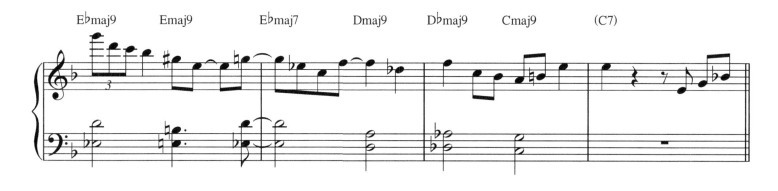

THELONIOUS

DISCOGRAPHY

Bemsha Swing – *Thelonious Monk Trio* (Prestige 7027-2)

Blue Monk – *Thelonious Monk Trio* (Prestige 7027-2)

Boo Boo's Birthday – *Underground* (Columbia Legacy CK-63535)

Criss Cross – *Criss-Cross* (Columbia Legacy CK-63537)

Epistrophy – *The Complete Riverside Recordings* (Riverside RCD-022-2)

I Mean You – *The Complete Blue Note Recordings* (Blue Note 30363)

In Walked Bud – *The Complete Blue Note Recordings* (Blue Note 30363)

Let's Cool One – *The Complete Riverside Recordings* (Riverside RCD-022-2)

Monk's Dream – *Thelonious Monk Trio* (Prestige 7027-2)

Nutty – *The Complete Riverside Recordings* (Riverside RCD-022-2)

Off Minor – *The Complete Blue Note Recordings* (Blue Note 30363)

Rhythm-a-ning – *Criss-Cross* (Columbia Legacy CK-63535)

Ruby, My Dear – *The Complete Blue Note Recordings* (Blue Note 30363)

Straight No Chaser – *Straight No Chaser* (Sony 64886)

Well You Needn't (It's Over Now) – *The Complete Blue Note Recordings* (Blue Note 30363)

ARTIST TRANSCRIPTIONS

Artist Transcriptions are authentic, note-for-note transcriptions of today's hottest artists in jazz, pop and rock. These outstanding, accurate arrangements are in an easy-to-read format which includes all essential lines. **Artist Transcriptions** can be used to perform, sequence or for reference.

CLARINET
00672423 Buddy De Franco Collection \$19.95

FLUTE
00672379 Eric Dolphy Collection............................\$19.95
00672582 The Very Best of James Galway \$16.99
00672372 James Moody Collection –
　　　　　Sax and Flute \$19.95

GUITAR & BASS
00660113 The Guitar Style of George Benson.......\$16.99
00699072 Guitar Book of Pierre Bensusan \$29.95
00672331 Ron Carter – Acoustic Bass..................\$19.99
00672573 Ray Brown – Legendary Jazz Bassist ..\$19.99
00672307 Stanley Clarke Collection......................\$19.99
00660115 Al Di Meola –
　　　　　Friday Night in San Francisco...............\$16.99
00604043 Al Di Meola –
　　　　　Music, Words, Pictures \$14.95
00672574 Al Di Meola –
　　　　　Pursuit of Radical Rhapsody \$22.99
00125617 Best of Herb Ellis \$19.99
00673245 Jazz Style of Tal Farlow \$19.99
00699306 Jim Hall – Exploring Jazz Guitar...........\$19.99
00604049 Allan Holdsworth –
　　　　　Reaching for the Uncommon Chord \$17.99
00699215 Leo Kottke – Eight Songs.....................\$17.99
00672353 Joe Pass Collection \$19.99
00673216 John Patitucci......................................\$17.99
00027083 Django Reinhardt Anthology \$16.99
00672374 Johnny Smith Guitar Solos....................\$19.99

PIANO & KEYBOARD
00672338 Monty Alexander Collection \$19.95
00672487 Monty Alexander Plays Standards \$19.95
00672520 Count Basie Collection \$19.95
00192307 Bebop Piano Legends............................\$19.99
00113680 Blues Piano Legends.............................\$19.99
00278003 A Charlie Brown Christmas..................\$17.99
00672439 Cyrus Chestnut Collection \$19.95
00672300 Chick Corea – Paint the World..............\$16.99
14037739 Storyville Presents Duke Ellington \$19.99
00146105 Bill Evans – Alone................................\$17.99
00672537 Bill Evans at Town Hall.........................\$19.99
00672548 The Mastery of Bill Evans \$16.99
00672425 Bill Evans – Piano Interpretations........\$22.99
00672365 Bill Evans – Piano Standards................\$19.99
00121885 Bill Evans – Time Remembered \$19.99
00672510 Bill Evans Trio – Vol. 1: 1959-1961 ....\$24.95
00672511 Bill Evans Trio – Vol. 2: 1962-1965........\$24.99
00672512 Bill Evans Trio – Vol. 3: 1968-1974........\$24.99
00672513 Bill Evans Trio – Vol. 4: 1979-1980 ....\$24.95
00672381 Tommy Flanagan Collection..................\$24.99
00193332 Erroll Garner – Concert by the Sea.......\$19.99
00672492 Benny Goodman Collection \$16.95
00672486 Vince Guaraldi Collection......................\$19.99
00672419 Herbie Hancock Collection....................\$19.95
00672438 Hampton Hawes \$19.95
14037738 Storyville Presents Earl Hines..............\$19.99

00672322 Ahmad Jamal Collection \$24.99
00255671 Jazz Piano Masterpieces......................\$19.99
00124367 Jazz Piano Masters Play
　　　　　Rodgers & Hammerstein \$19.99
00672564 Best of Jeff Lorber..............................\$17.99
00672476 Brad Mehldau Collection \$19.99
00672388 Best of Thelonious Monk \$19.95
00672389 Thelonious Monk Collection \$22.99
00672390 Thelonious Monk Plays
　　　　　Jazz Standards – Volume 1 ....\$19.99
00672391 Thelonious Monk Plays
　　　　　Jazz Standards – Volume 2 ....\$19.95
00672433 Jelly Roll Morton – The Piano Rolls \$16.99
00672553 Charlie Parker for Piano........................\$19.95
00672542 Oscar Peterson – Jazz Piano Solos..... \$17.99
00672562 Oscar Peterson –
　　　　　A Jazz Portrait of Frank Sinatra............\$19.95
00264094 Oscar Peterson – Night Train \$19.99
00672544 Oscar Peterson – Originals...................\$10.99
00672532 Oscar Peterson – Plays Broadway........\$19.95
00672531 Oscar Peterson –
　　　　　Plays Duke Ellington \$24.99
00672563 Oscar Peterson –
　　　　　A Royal Wedding Suite \$19.99
00672569 Oscar Peterson – Tracks......................\$19.99
00672533 Oscar Peterson – Trios.........................\$24.95
00672543 Oscar Peterson Trio –
　　　　　Canadiana Suite \$12.99
00672534 Very Best of Oscar Peterson...............\$22.95
00672371 Bud Powell Classics.............................\$19.99
00672376 Bud Powell Collection...........................\$19.95
00672507 Gonzalo Rubalcaba Collection \$19.95
00672303 Horace Silver Collection........................\$22.99
00672316 Art Tatum Collection \$24.99
00672355 Art Tatum Solo Book \$19.95
00673215 McCoy Tyner \$19.99
00672321 Cedar Walton Collection \$19.95
00672519 Kenny Werner Collection.......................\$19.95
00672434 Teddy Wilson Collection........................\$19.95

SAXOPHONE
00672566 The Mindi Abair Collection \$14.99
00673244 Julian "Cannonball"
　　　　　Adderley Collection..............................\$19.95
00673237 Michael Brecker \$19.95
00672429 Michael Brecker Collection \$22.99
00672315 Benny Carter Plays Standards.............\$22.95
00672394 James Carter Collection........................\$19.95
00672349 John Coltrane Plays Giant Steps \$19.95
00672529 John Coltrane – Giant Steps.................\$17.99
00672494 John Coltrane – A Love Supreme........\$15.99
00307393 John Coltrane –
　　　　　Omnibook: C Instruments \$24.99
00307391 John Coltrane –
　　　　　Omnibook: B-flat Instruments \$27.99
00307392 John Coltrane –
　　　　　Omnibook: E-flat Instruments \$29.99
00307394 John Coltrane –
　　　　　Omnibook: Bass Clef Instruments \$24.99

00672493 John Coltrane
　　　　　Plays "Coltrane Changes"....................\$19.95
00672453 John Coltrane Plays Standards............\$22.99
00673233 John Coltrane Solos \$22.95
00672328 Paul Desmond Collection \$19.99
00672379 Eric Dolphy Collection...........................\$19.95
00672530 Kenny Garrett Collection \$19.95
00699375 Stan Getz...\$19.99
00672377 Stan Getz – Bossa Novas \$22.99
00672375 Stan Getz – Standards.........................\$19.99
00673254 Great Tenor Sax Solos.........................\$18.99
00672523 Coleman Hawkins Collection \$19.99
00673252 Joe Henderson – Selections from
　　　　　"Lush Life" & "So Near So Far"............\$19.95
00673239 Best of Kenny G....................................\$19.95
00673229 Kenny G – Breathless \$19.95
00672462 Kenny G – Classics in the Key of G \$19.95
00672485 Kenny G – Faith: A Holiday Album \$15.99
00672373 Kenny G – The Moment........................\$19.95
00672498 Jackie McLean Collection \$19.95
00672372 James Moody Collection –
　　　　　Sax and Flute \$19.95
00672416 Frank Morgan Collection \$19.95
00672539 Gerry Mulligan Collection......................\$19.95
00672352 Charlie Parker Collection \$19.95
00672561 Best of Sonny Rollins............................\$19.95
00102751 Sonny Rollins
　　　　　with the Modern Jazz Quartet \$17.99
00675000 David Sanborn Collection \$19.99
00672491 New Best of Wayne Shorter.................\$22.99
00672550 The Sonny Stitt Collection....................\$19.95
00672524 Lester Young Collection.........................\$19.99

TROMBONE
00672332 J.J. Johnson Collection \$19.99
00672489 Steve Turré Collection \$19.99

TRUMPET
00672557 Herb Alpert Collection \$17.99
00672480 Louis Armstrong Collection \$19.99
00672481 Louis Armstrong Plays Standards........ \$19.99
00672435 Chet Baker Collection \$19.99
00672556 Best of Chris Botti \$19.99
00672448 Miles Davis – Originals, Vol. 1...............\$19.99
00672451 Miles Davis – Originals, Vol. 2...............\$19.99
00672450 Miles Davis – Standards, Vol. 1 ....\$19.9
00672449 Miles Davis – Standards, Vol. 2 ....\$19.9
00672479 Dizzy Gillespie Collection \$19.9
00673214 Freddie Hubbard \$19.9
00672382 Tom Harrell – Jazz Trumpet \$19.9
00672363 Jazz Trumpet Solos..............................\$9.9
00672506 Chuck Mangione Collection \$19.9
00672525 Arturo Sandoval – Trumpet Evolution....\$19.9